The Wild Midwest

MARK MÜLLER *University of Iowa Press • Iowa City*

University of Iowa Press, Iowa City 52242

www.uiowapress.org
Printed in the United States of America

Design by April Leidig

The University of Iowa Press is a member of Green Press Initiative
and is committed to preserving natural resources.

Printed on acid-free paper

ISBN: 978-1-60938-469-2 (pbk)

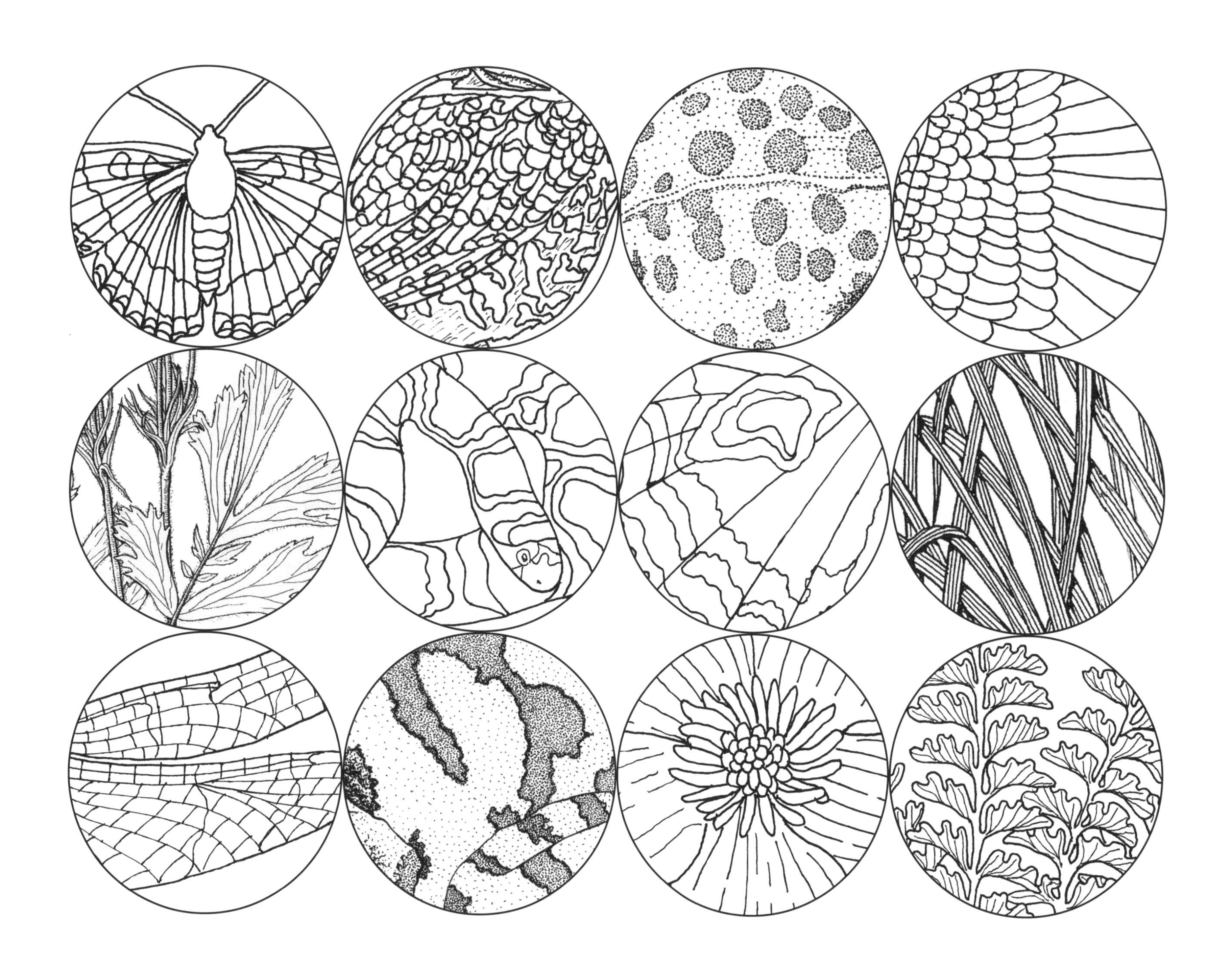

Bambi and blue flag iris

For decades midwesterners would ooh and ahh when they spotted a white-tailed deer, but now they say, "Oh no, there goes my garden!" Deer have adapted so well to this agricultural landscape that their numbers are at record levels, and they have become an overpopulated nuisance in some areas.

Top, left to right: luna moth, bronze copper, meadow fritillary; center, left to right: Melissa blue, Milbert's tortoiseshell, Reakirt's blue; bottom, left to right: olive hairstreak, regal fritillary, Olympia marble

Butterflies and moths not only grace our world with beauty but are important pollinators as well. They aren't as dainty as they look and can put in a long day's (or night's, in the case of moths) work just as well as a hardy farmer.

Left to right: pale purple coneflower,
gray-headed coneflower

Coneflowers are easy-to-grow native prairie plants. But being a commoner doesn't mean they should be taken for granted — they are just as important and beautiful as the rare dandies.

Northern painted turtle

For decades in the past, pet stores sold baby turtles, but turtles have an eclectic diet — one we humans don't have a menu for — and most died and were flushed down the toilet. Fortunately laws now forbid selling turtles — except the tasty chocolate and caramel ones.

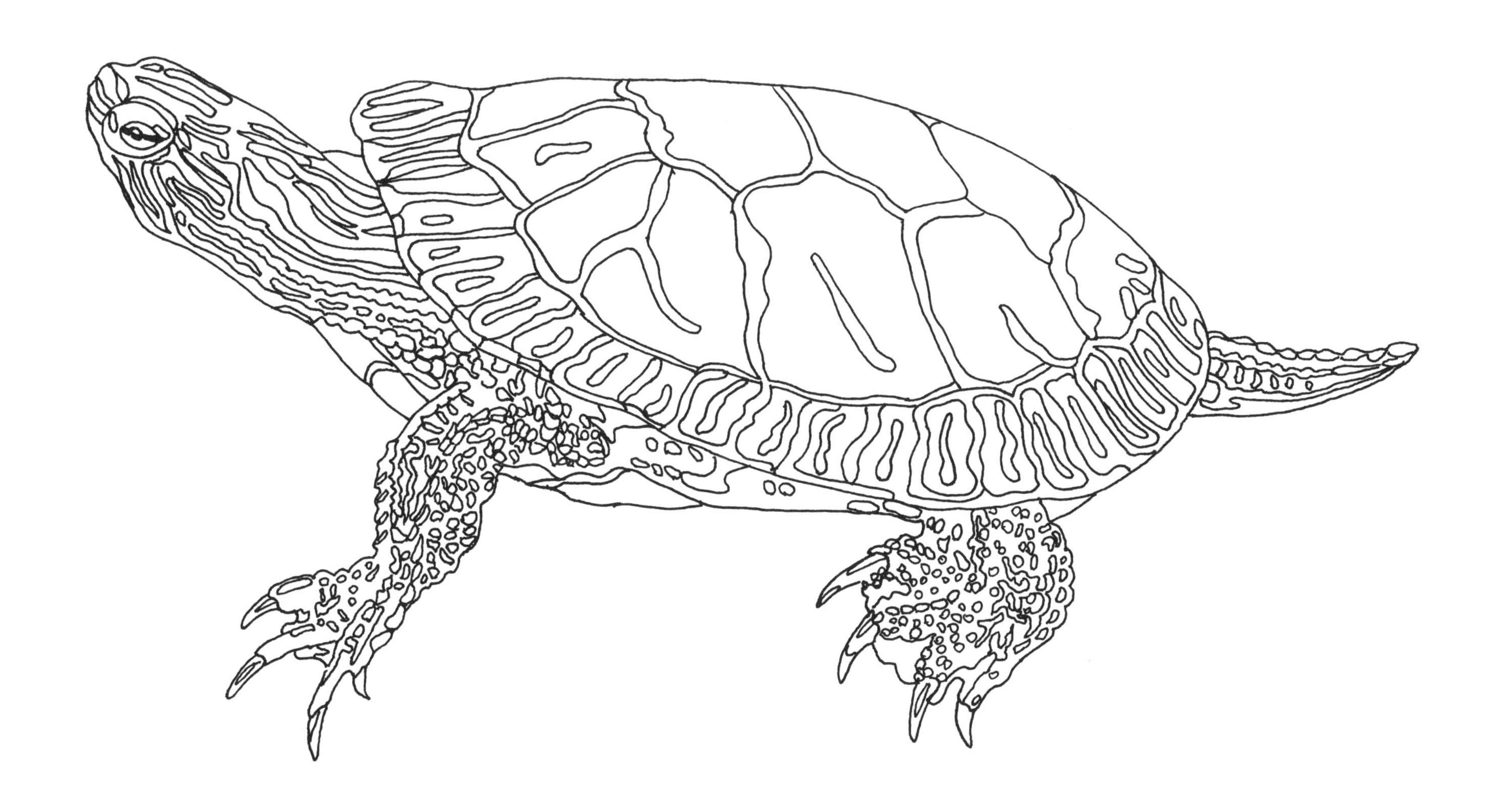

Greater prairie-chickens

Millions of greater prairie-chickens once danced and boomed on midwestern prairies. These birds were also tasty and easy to trap or shoot. Market hunters would kill thousands in a day and sell them for about fifty cents each.

Left to right: North American river otter, northern flying squirrel, cougar

Otters can be found in rivers and lakes, flying squirrels glide in mature woodlands, and cougars — also called pumas or mountain lions — sometimes lounge on a tree limb in a suburban backyard, which can add a bit of excitement to wildlife viewing.

Left to right: cinnamon fern, maidenhair fern, ladyfern

Ferns are nonflowering plants with flair. Graceful plants with delicate fronds and leaflets, they are found mostly in woodlands, but there are a few prairie species as well.

Canada goose and goslings

Canada geese, like white-tailed deer, have adapted so well to urban areas that they are considered a nuisance. Maybe we should resurrect the big, easy-to-catch, and tasty concept for some species.

Clockwise from upper left: northern spring peeper, gray treefrog, northern leopard frog, plains leopard frog

Amphibians are reliable indicators of the health of an ecosystem. They tend to breathe through their skin and thus absorb anything in their environment — including the toxins that we discard. A frog with an extra set of hind legs is a sad sight.

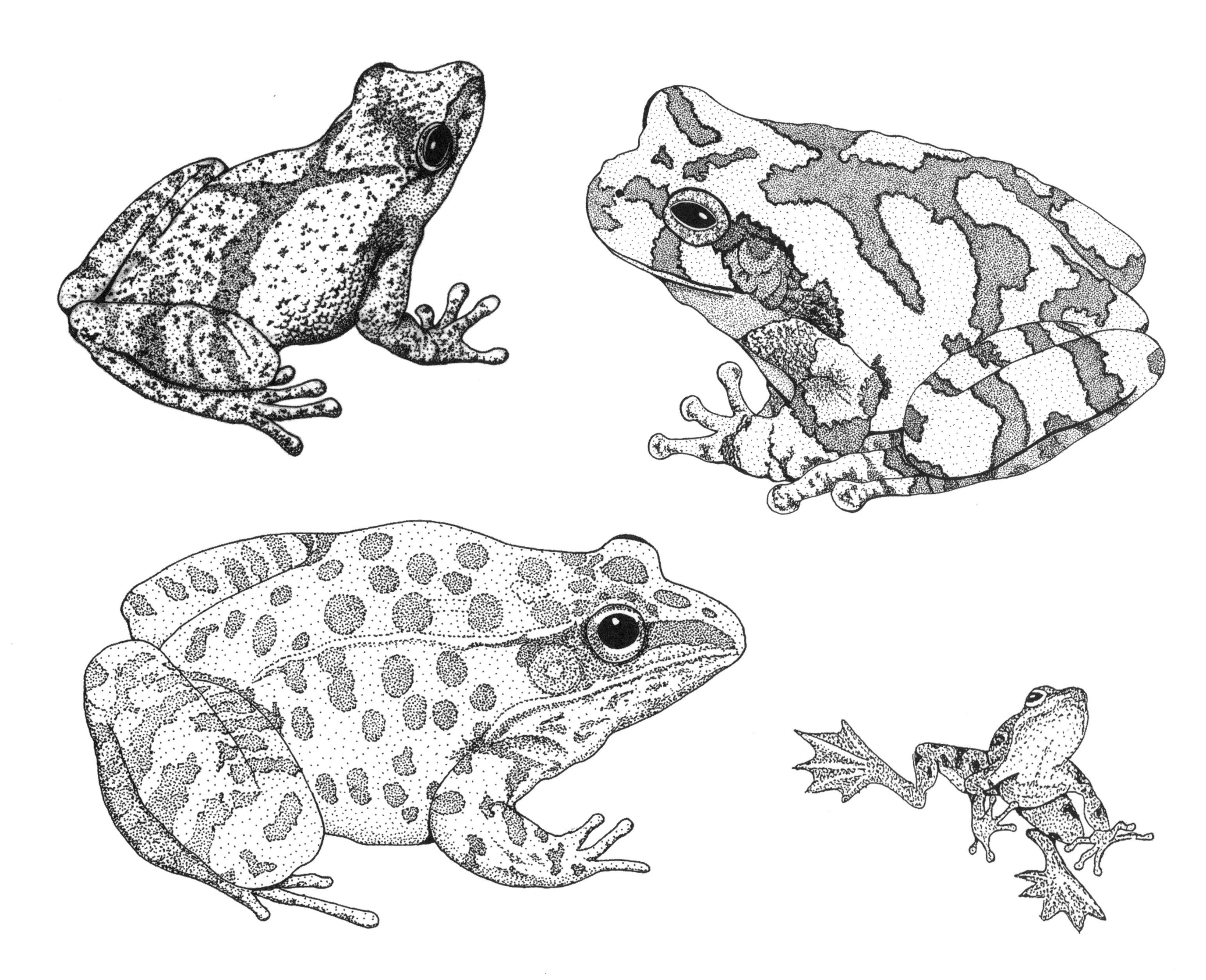

Left to right: shooting stars, prairie smoke

Shooting stars and prairie smoke can be difficult to establish but add a brilliant splash of early-spring color to a prairie planting. Neither one shoots or smokes.

Clockwise from upper left: eastern pondhawk, eastern amberwing, widow skimmer

By feasting heavily on mosquitoes, dragonflies and their larvae are drones with a benevolent task that benefits all of humanity and defies the Federal Aviation Administration. They have a strike-and-kill success rate greater than 90 percent.

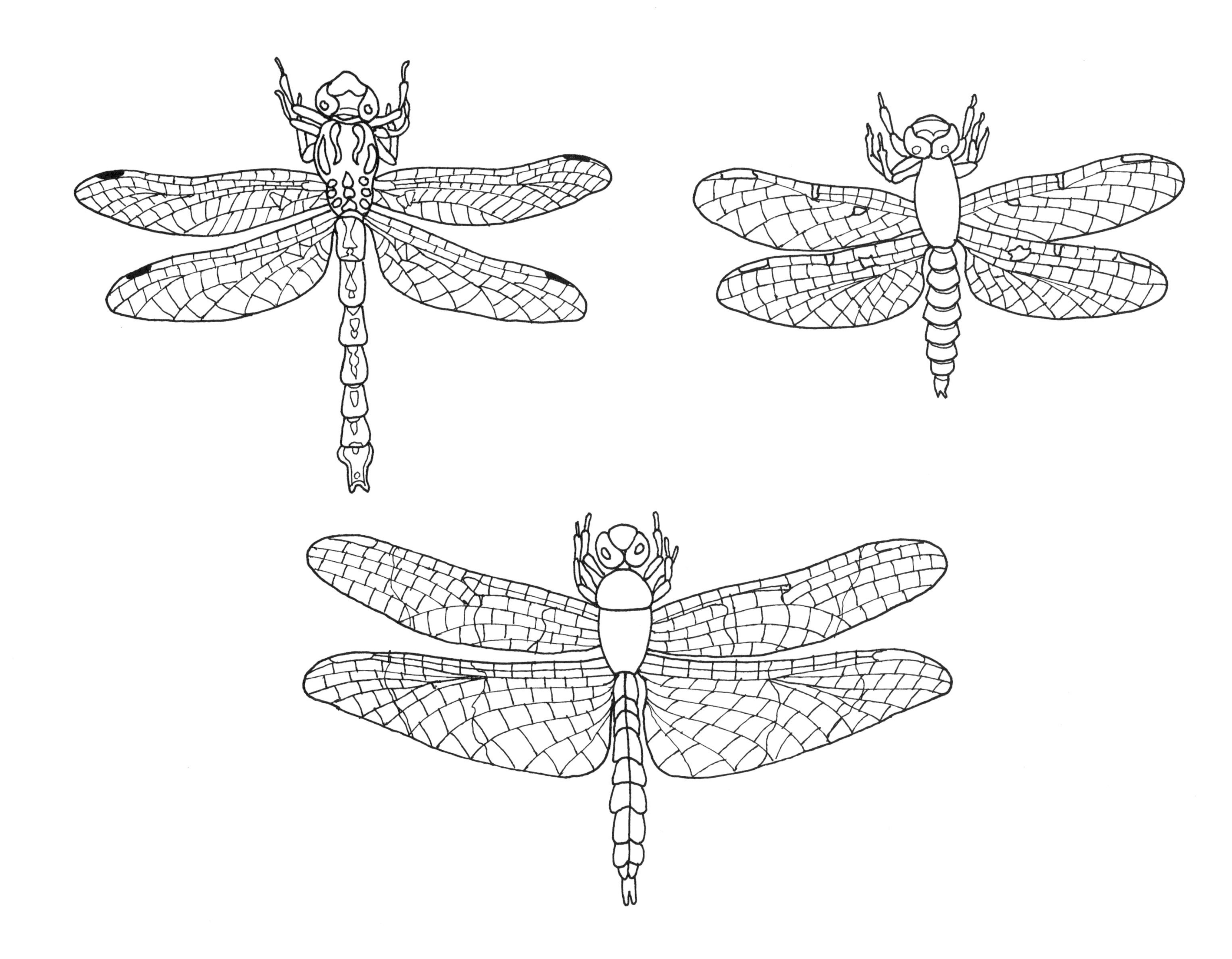

Elk

Elk (or *wapiti*) were a common sight on midwestern prairies presettlement. Of course, they were big, tasty targets, so they didn't last long after European pioneers arrived.

Belted kingfisher

Kingfishers spot fish while hovering above a lake or stream, then plunge head first into the water to nab their meal. They often fly to a perch and beat their prey into submission on a branch before swallowing it whole.

Cecropia moth

Cecropia moths are night fliers and do not feed as adults. They have wild sex for one night and then die; the female lays her eggs before expiring. Cecropias are one of the largest moths, with wingspans up to six inches.

Top: six-lined racerunner; bottom: milk snake

Reptiles are cold-blooded creatures that need warm days to get them up and going. It's understandable for people to be wary of a twelve-foot-long alligator, but it's silly to scream when encountering a six-inch-long garter snake. They're cool.

Left to right: small-flowered lady's-slipper, nodding ladies'-tresses, western prairie fringed orchid

Prairie orchids are all rare, and it's a stroke of fine luck if you happen upon one. If you do, please leave it alone. It's so tempting to covet one for your flower garden, but they do not transplant. Just enjoy the moment.

Left to right: burrowing owl, barn owl, short-eared owl

Owls are usually nocturnal with extremely sensitive hearing and eyesight adapted for dark conditions. They are not able to spin their heads 360 degrees, but it sure seems like it when they quickly look from side to side.

Nonflowering woodland plants

Nonflowering plants such as fungi, moss, scouring rush, and lichens are often found in woodlands on rotting logs or stumps. They tend to be a tad drab and are certainly underappreciated for their skill in breaking down and recycling dead stuff. Some fungi are quite delicious.

Clockwise from upper left: white-tailed deer, American bison, moose, white-tailed jackrabbit, fox squirrel, porcupine

Mammals of the Midwest come in a variety of sizes ranging from tiny shrews — the smallest mammals — to towering bison. Moose, deer, and bison suffered the same big-and-tasty fate as elk once hungry settlers arrived.

Left to right: western meadowlark, eastern meadowlark

Western and eastern meadowlarks are nearly identical, but their songs are quite different. My friend Peter Lowther thinks that the eastern sounds like part of Beethoven's 6th Symphony and the western sounds more like a bubbly gurgle.

Clockwise from upper left: bur oak, sugar maple, black walnut, northern red oak, hackberry, shagbark hickory leaves and nuts

Many creatures depend upon the leaves, nuts, and fruits of trees for survival. Decade after decade, we have planted monocultures like the American elm that can be wiped out in short order by disease. Now ash trees are susceptible to the same fate via the emerald ash borer. Think diversity!

Butterfly garden

Butterflies can't resist a garden with a variety of flowering plants, access to water, and spots for resting. If you build it they will come, but if your yard is a monoculture of bluegrass, don't expect many colorful visitors.

Left to right: butterfly milkweed, monarch, common milkweed

Adult monarchs sip on nectar from all kinds of flowers, but their larvae feed only on milkweed plants. Our use of herbicides has nearly wiped out milkweeds in and around farm fields and along roadsides, causing the monarch population to crash.

Left to right: green heron, great blue heron

Herons are more patient than most human fishers. They stand as still as a statue in the shallows, then spear small fish with lightning speed. Occasionally they try to eat something bigger than their head, with unfortunate results.

Caterpillar garden

The key to attracting wildlife is a diversity of plants. Caterpillars often prefer to feed on specific species. If nothing is moving in your yard except a lawnmower, maybe it's time for a landscape alteration.

Clockwise from upper left: spotted lady beetle, American burying beetle, American stag beetle

There are more different species of beetles than nearly all the other species of critters combined — more than 25,000 in North America alone. They're not cars, and they're not capable of producing top-40 hits, but they are vital components of a healthy ecosystem.

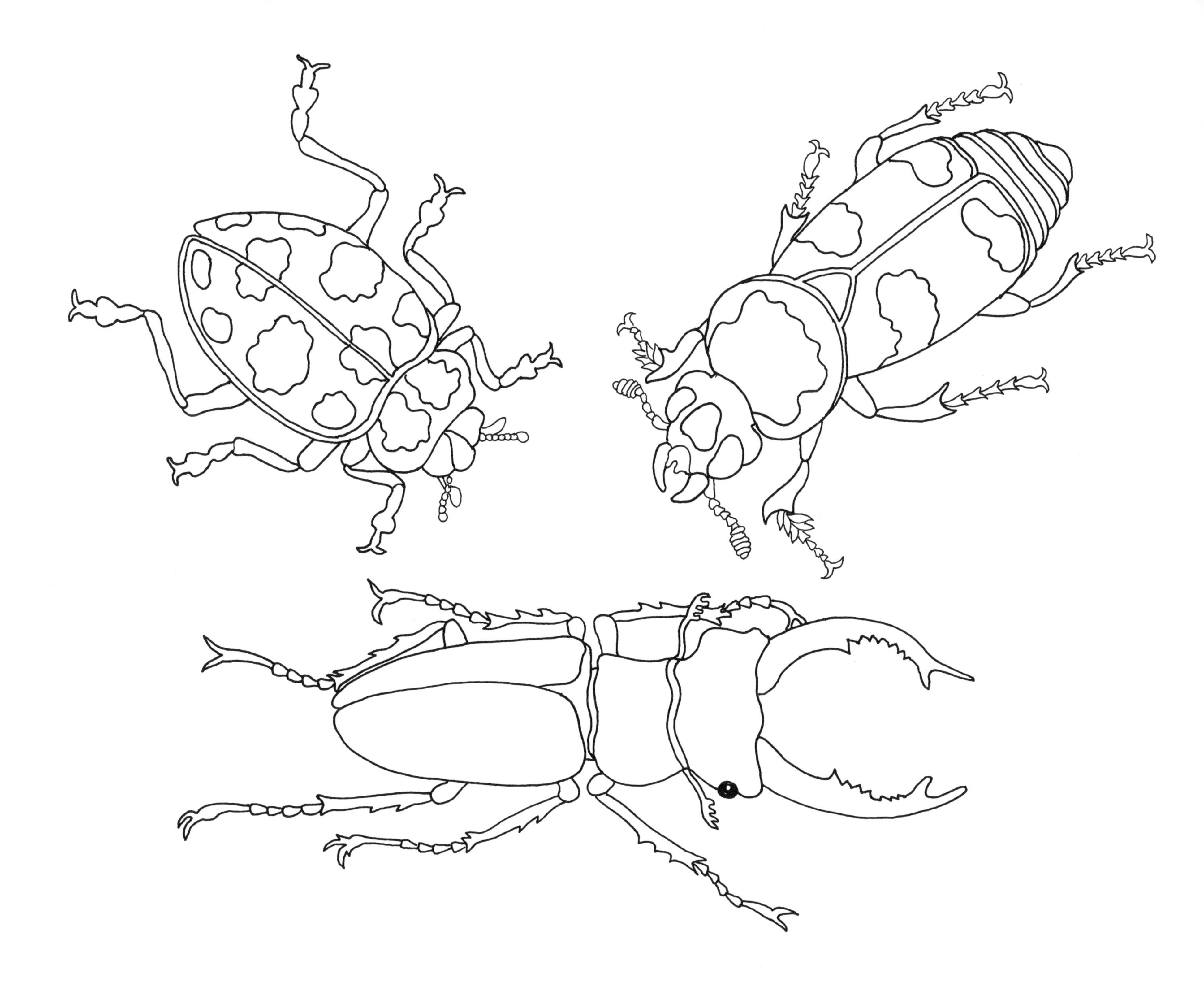

Wetland

Wetlands are complex, endangered ecosystems with a high diversity of wildlife. They are often reviled as dark, sinister swamps in books and movies, but they are fantastic water filters and full of bright, colorful, harmless characters like this muskrat.

Left to right: yellow lady's-slipper, showy lady's-slipper

Woodland orchids are as rare as prairie orchids and just as exquisite. Just because you are less conspicuous in a woodland than an open prairie, don't be tempted to dig one up. It will die.

Top to bottom: walleye, northern pike, largemouth bass

Walleye, northerns, and bass are ferocious hunters, eating anything they can catch, but being another tasty species, they are no match for a human with a little common sense and a fishing pole.

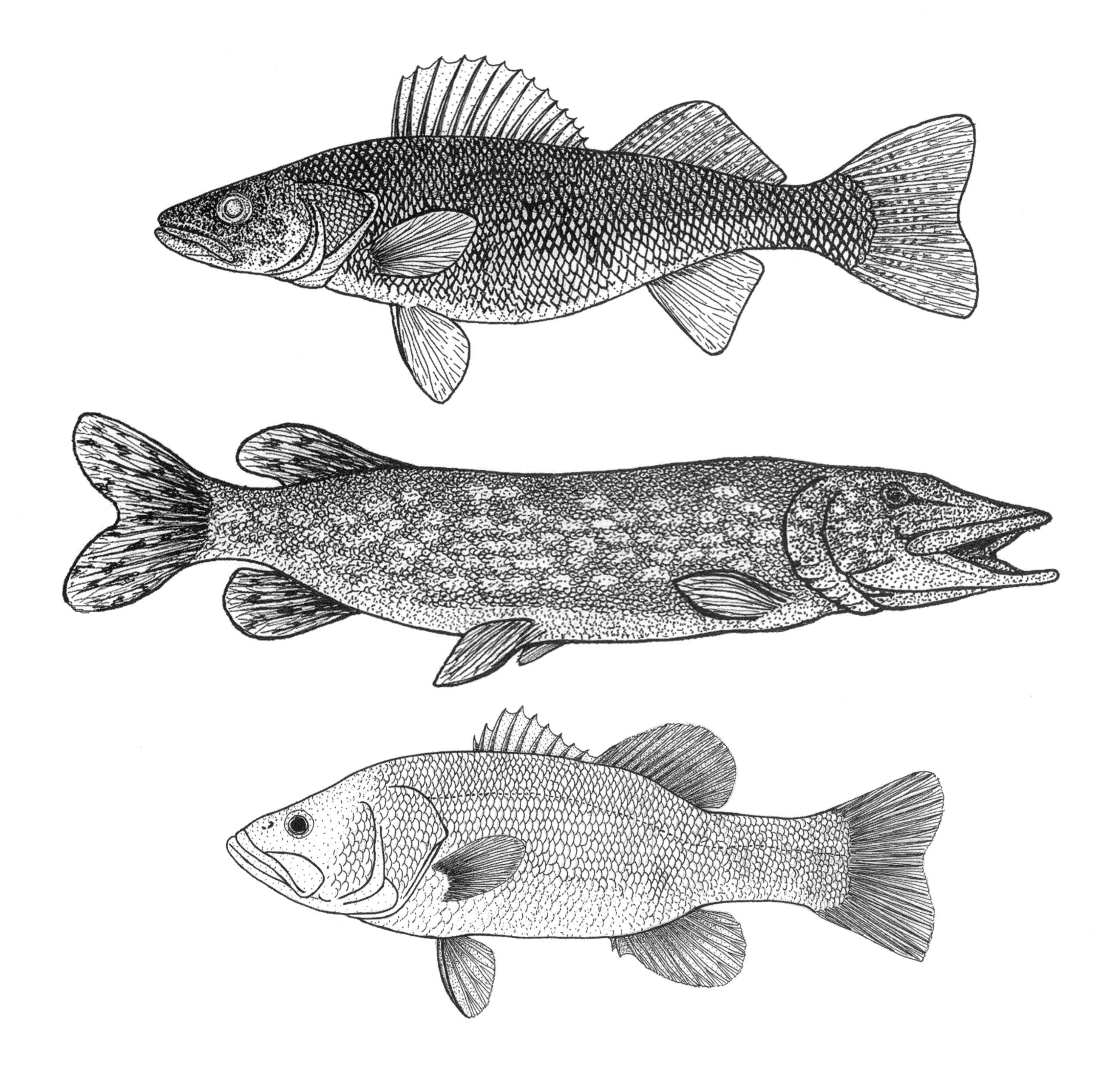

Left to right: American kestrel, bald eagle, Cooper's hawk

Midwestern raptors include hawks, falcons, eagles, owls, and vultures, all top predators in the food web. If it weren't for raptors, we would be up to our necks in rodents. For decades anyone who killed these "varmints" was paid a government bounty. We now know how stupid that was.

Top, left to right: bloodroot, nightshade, large white trillium; bottom, left to right: Dutchman's breeches, marsh marigold, trout lily

Woodland wildflowers are at their showiest when the spring ephemerals are in bloom. Given that many of them have names like liverleaf, skunk cabbage, carrion flower, and toothwort, you'll be pleasantly surprised by their beauty.

Clockwise from upper left: larva and adult emerald ash borer, mature garlic mustard with seed pod, Asian longhorned beetle, Japanese beetle, first-year garlic mustard, adult and larva gypsy moth

Because invasive species usually arrive from other countries, they often have no predators in their new home to control them. They compete with and sometimes overwhelm native species. This sounds like a perfect description of the mightiest species ever to invade this continent: humans.

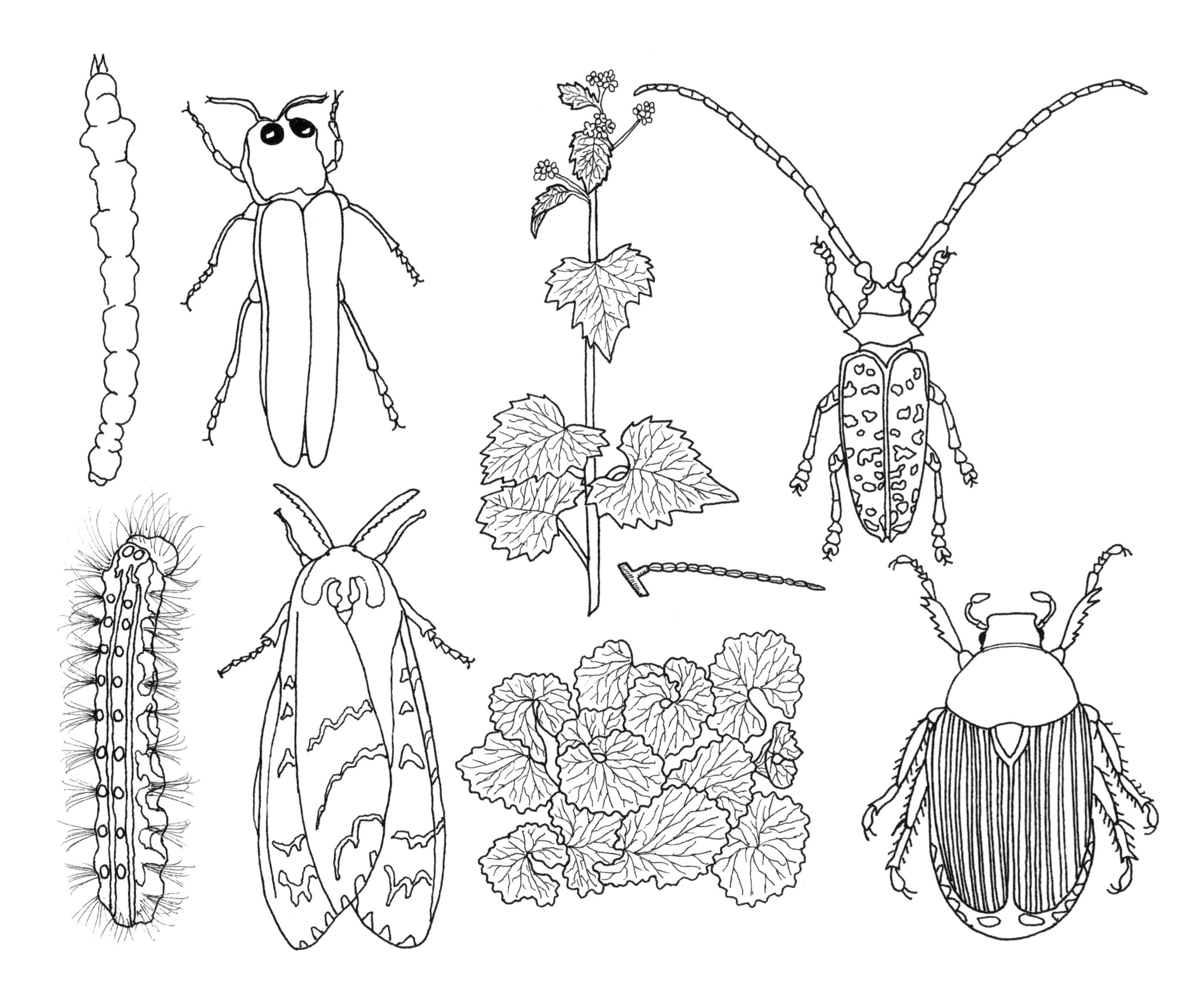

Cycle of Life

Everything in nature is interconnected, like an elaborate tapestry. If you start pulling on just one thread, you will eventually dismantle the whole thing and end up with a huge mess.